# The Comedy of Errors

## Shakespeare for Kids

Written for kids by Jeanette Vigon

Adapted from the works of William Shakespeare

This book is a modern adaptation for children of William Shakespeare's " The Comedy of Errors," which is a work in the public domain. While the original story and characters are based on Shakespeare's play, this adaptation includes significant original content tailored for a young audience. These additions include simplified language and reimagined scenes, specifically created to make this profound tale accessible and engaging for young readers. The intention of this adaptation is to introduce children to the classic story in a manner that respects the essence of Shakespeare's original work, while presenting it in a way that is relatable and understandable for a younger audience.

# A NOTE FOR PARENTS: ADAPTING " THE COMEDY OF ERRORS" AND THE ESSENCE OF SHAKESPEARE FOR YOUNG READERS

Embarking on the journey to adapt William Shakespeare's "The Comedy of Errors" for young readers has been an exhilarating challenge, driven by the goal of bridging the rich tales of Shakespeare with the vivid imaginations of children. My primary ambition is to introduce them to the grandeur of classical literature early on, fostering a lifelong appreciation for storytelling.

## Addressing the Content and Language for Children

"The Comedy of Errors," celebrated for its humorous storyline and intricate plot of mistaken identities, presents complexities including themes of family, identity, and the chaos of misunderstandings. Adapting these themes for a younger audience necessitated a thoughtful approach to simplify the language and situations without losing the essence of Shakespeare's original genius. My objective was to captivate young minds, making the story both accessible and engaging.

## Preserving Shakespeare's Integrity

Choosing to keep the original act and scene structure intact was a deliberate decision to honor the rhythm and structural beauty of Shakespeare's work. This strategy not only pays homage to the original play but also introduces young readers to the sophistication of narrative structure and dramatic conventions. It is essential for children to experience the play as Shakespeare imagined it, yet in a form that is inviting to them.

## Themes Tailored for a Young Audience

The adaptation of "The Comedy of Errors" involved careful consideration of content, ensuring that its themes of mistaken identity, the importance of family, and the joy of reunification were conveyed in a manner that is both educational and appealing to children. The comedic elements and the ethical dilemmas the play presents were carefully balanced to highlight values of empathy, patience, and the significance of understanding and forgiveness.

## Why This Adaptation Matters

This adaptation stems from a passion to make Shakespeare's works accessible to audiences of all ages, especially children, in the hope of instilling an early love for classic literature. I believe that by introducing these stories to children, we lay the groundwork for a lifelong engagement with reading and appreciation for the arts. The choice to adapt "The Comedy of Errors" for young readers arises from a desire to immerse them in the beauty of literature from a tender age, encouraging an enduring fondness for reading.

Crafting this adaptation was a journey fueled by enthusiasm, committed to ensuring that the humor and joy of Shakespeare's story resonate with young readers. It was an endeavor in preserving the heart of the play while making it suitable for children, with the aspiration that it will kindle a passion for timeless literature in their hearts.

I hope that you and your young readers find as much delight in exploring this adaptation as I did in reimagining it for them, inviting them into the vast and marvelous world of Shakespeare's plays, adapted to enrich their youthful minds and spirits.

# INTRODUCTION TO " THE COMEDY OF ERRORS"

Welcome to the bustling streets of Ephesus, a place brimming with enchantment, mistaken identities, and a whirlwind of comedic situations. This isn't just a story; it's a hilarious journey through the confusion of two sets of twins, separated at birth, whose paths cross in a series of uproarious misunderstandings and delightful coincidences.

Our adventure is set in a city alive with commerce, intrigue, and magic, where every corner and shadow may conceal a new twist or a bewildering encounter. In this lively setting, a cast of characters finds themselves entangled in a plot filled with mistaken identities, misplaced affections, and mischievous escapades.

At the center of our tale are two pairs of twins—Antipholus of Syracuse and Antipholus of Ephesus, and their servants, both named Dromio. Unaware of each other's presence in Ephesus, their accidental encounters with the city's inhabitants lead to a series of comedic misunderstandings, accusations of infidelity, theft, and even madness. But this is no mere comedy of errors; it's a heartwarming exploration of identity, family, and the joy of reunion.

Fear not, for amidst the chaos and confusion, there are moments of laughter, love, and light-heartedness. The Dromios, with their witty banter and slapstick humor, teach us about loyalty and the joys of friendship, while the reunion of the twins and their families reminds us of the enduring bonds of family and the happiness of finding one's other half.

So, prepare yourselves for an expedition to "The Comedy of Errors," where every mistaken identity and comedic twist takes us deeper into the heart of its characters. Imagine a world where every encounter could lead to a new confusion, where every dialogue is a potential for laughter, and where a day filled with errors leads to the ultimate discovery of familial love and unity.

Are you ready? Then let's dive into the vibrant streets of Ephesus, with its mistaken twins, bewildered townsfolk, and unexpected reunions. Immerse yourself in a tale that has delighted audiences for centuries, now reimagined to captivate and amuse the young and the young at heart. Here we go, into the uproarious world of "The Comedy of Errors," where every mix-up spins a tale of humor, and every resolution lights the way to a joyous reunion!

# ACT I

# SCENE 1

In the grand hall of Duke Solinus's palace, Duke Solinus, Aegon, and some officers and attendants gathered around. Aegon, a visitor from Syracuse, was in a bit of trouble.

Aegon pleaded, "Please, Solinus, let's end this quickly and put an end to my suffering."

Duke Solinus responded firmly, "Merchant from Syracuse, I cannot bend our laws for you. Our cities have been fighting, and because of the trouble your people have caused, our laws have become very strict. Anyone from Syracuse caught in our city, Ephesus, will be punished severely, even with death, unless they can pay a big fine. Unfortunately, you don't have enough to pay this fine, so by our laws, you are sentenced to die."

Aegon sighed, "At least when your decision is made, my troubles will end with the day."

Duke Solinus, curious, asked, "Tell me, why did you leave your home in Syracuse, and why did you come to Ephesus?"

This was the beginning of Aegon's story, where he would explain his reasons, hoping for some understanding or perhaps mercy from the Duke.

Aegon continued to share his heartbreaking story, his voice heavy with sorrow. "Talking about my deep sadness is the hardest task. I was born in Syracuse and married a wonderful woman. Our happiness grew alongside our wealth from my many successful trips to Epidamnum. However, after the death of my business partner and the chaotic state of my affairs, I had to leave my wife behind. She followed me shortly after, despite being close to giving birth. And soon, she joyfully brought two identical twin boys into the world. At the same time, another woman gave birth to twin boys as well. These twins, born to a less fortunate family, were taken in by us to be companions to our sons."

"Our family was complete, and my wife longed for us to return home. Reluctantly, I agreed. But our journey back turned perilous as a storm hit. The sea turned against us, and we lost all hope of survival. My wife and I did our best to protect our children, tying them and ourselves to a mast to avoid being separated by the waves. Eventually, we were rescued, but the ordeal wasn't over. The ships that came to our aid were from Corinth and Epidaurus. But before they could reach us, my tale takes a turn. I'll leave the rest to your imagination."

Duke Solinus, touched by the story, urged, "Please, continue. Your tale, while sad, may not free you from punishment, but it earns our sympathy."

Aegon, with a heavy heart, shared the final part of his tale. "If only the gods had been kinder, I wouldn't call them merciless now. Before we could reach the ships coming to rescue us, a giant rock struck us. Our ship broke in two, separating my family. My wife and one of our sons were picked up by fishermen from Corinth, or so we thought. Another ship rescued me and my remaining son. They tried to reunite us with my wife and other son, but couldn't catch up to the fishermen's slower boat. So, we headed home, separated from our loved ones."

"Years passed, and my youngest son, filled with a longing to find his brother, convinced me to let him search. We traveled far and wide, hoping to find them. Eventually, we came to Ephesus, but found no trace of them. Now, it seems my journey ends here, in Ephesus, with my life at risk."

Duke Solinus responded with sympathy, "Aegon, fate has indeed been harsh to you. If it weren't for the laws of our land, I'd help you. But I can't go against the laws. However, I'll give you until the end of the day to find the money to save your life. Try to find help in Ephesus. If you can't, then I'm afraid the law must take its course."

With that, the jailer took Aegon away, leaving him to find a way to extend his life, even if just for a little while longer.

# SCENE 2

In the busy market, Antipholus of Syracuse and his servant Dromio, along with a friendly merchant, discussed their situation. The merchant advised, "You should pretend you're from Epidamnum, so your things aren't taken away. Today, a merchant from Syracuse was caught and couldn't pay the fine to save his life. He won't see the sunset. Here's your money."

Antipholus instructed, "Take this money to our inn, the Centaur, and wait for me, Dromio. I'll explore the town and meet you later."

Dromio agreed, "Alright, I'll go now," and left.

Antipholus then shared, "Dromio often cheers me up with his jokes when I'm feeling down."

He invited the merchant, "Would you like to explore the town with me, then dine at my inn?"

The merchant declined, "I have plans with some merchants, but let's meet later at the market and spend the evening together. I must go now."

"See you later, then," said Antipholus, planning to wander the town alone. "He tells me to enjoy myself, but that's hard when I'm searching for my family, feeling lost in this big world."

Just then, Dromio of Ephesus appeared, surprising Antipholus. "Why are you back so soon?" he asked, not realizing this was a different Dromio.

Dromio of Ephesus, mistaking Antipholus of Syracuse for his master, hurriedly explained, "I'm not early; I'm actually late! Dinner's ruined back at home; the food's cold, and my mistress is upset because of it. She blames me, saying it's cold because you haven't come home."

Antipholus, confused, asked, "Hold on, where's the money I gave you?"

Dromio of Ephesus, puzzled, replied, "Money? You mean the sixpence for the saddler? I paid him; I didn't keep it."

Antipholus, growing frustrated, pressed, "I'm serious. Where is the money? It's risky to misplace such a large amount, especially since we're strangers here."

Dromio, misunderstanding the question, continued, "I came quickly from my mistress, asking you to come home for dinner. If I go back empty-handed, she'll be furious with me."

Antipholus, trying to keep calm, said, "Enough with the jokes. Where did you put the gold I entrusted to you?"

Dromio, still confused, answered, "Gold? You didn't give me any gold."

Antipholus, now quite irritated, demanded, "Stop playing around and tell me what you did with the money."

Dromio, innocently, explained, "I was just supposed to bring you home from the market to our house, the Phoenix, for dinner. My mistress and her sister are waiting for you."

This mix-up led to a humorous misunderstanding, as Antipholus of Syracuse had never met this Dromio or his supposed "mistress."

Antipholus of Syracuse grew more frustrated, demanding to know where his money was hidden. "Tell me where you've kept my money, or I'll make you regret your tricks!"

Dromio of Ephesus, feeling misunderstood and mistreated, replied, "I've got plenty of marks from you and my mistress, but certainly not a thousand marks. If I were to give those back, you might not be too happy."

Antipholus, confused and angry, asked, "What mistress are you talking about?"

Dromio explained, "Your wife, my mistress at the Phoenix. She's waiting for you to come home for dinner."

Antipholus, feeling mocked, couldn't believe what he was hearing and threatened Dromio, who then decided to flee, fearing more misunderstanding.

Left alone, Antipholus of Syracuse mused on the possibility of being cheated out of his money in this strange town, known for its tricksters and deceivers. Worried about his safety and his money, he resolved to find this mysterious servant at the Centaur inn and get to the bottom of things.

# ACT II

# SCENE 1

In the house of Antipholus of Ephesus, Adriana and her sister Luciana were having a conversation. Adriana was worried because her husband hadn't returned home, even though she had sent a servant to find him.

"It's already two o'clock, and neither my husband nor the servant has come back," Adriana said, clearly upset.

Luciana tried to calm her down, suggesting, "Maybe a friend invited him over, and he's out having lunch. Let's not worry too much. We should have our meal and wait patiently. Men like to feel free to do as they please, and they'll come home when they're ready."

"But why should they have more freedom than we do?" Adriana questioned, not satisfied with the situation.

Luciana explained, "Their work often requires them to be outside. But remember, your happiness shouldn't depend solely on what he does."

Adriana expressed her frustration, "Whenever I try to do something nice for him, he doesn't appreciate it."

Luciana offered some wisdom, "Think of it this way: being patient and understanding is how you guide him."

Adriana wasn't convinced, "I don't think anyone should be controlled like that."

Luciana continued, "But sometimes, having too much freedom can lead to trouble. Everything in this world, including animals and birds, follows certain rules. Men, who are capable of great things, also have responsibilities, especially in taking care of their families."

"That's exactly why I don't want to get married," Adriana replied, thinking about the challenges of marriage.

"It's not marriage that's the problem, but the difficulties that come with it," Luciana corrected her.

"If I were married, I'd want to have a say in things," Adriana insisted.

"Before I think about love, I'll learn to follow and understand," Luciana said thoughtfully.

"And what if your husband turns his attention elsewhere?" Adriana asked, bringing up another concern.

As Luciana and Adriana continued their discussion, Luciana mentioned she would wait for the right time to marry, emphasizing the importance of patience. Just then, Dromio of Ephesus arrived, interrupting their conversation.

"Have you seen your master? Is he on his way home?" Adriana asked Dromio eagerly.

"Well, he's been giving me a hard time, that's for sure," Dromio replied, hinting at a rough encounter.

"Did you talk to him? Do you know what he's thinking?" Adriana pressed on, hoping for good news.

"Yes, I did, but his message was as tough as his punches," Dromio said, implying that his conversation with his master was anything but pleasant.

Luciana, puzzled, asked, "Was he speaking so unclearly that you couldn't understand him?"

"No, his message was loud and clear, especially the part where he hit me," Dromio explained, trying to lighten the mood with his misfortune.

"But is he coming home for dinner? It seems like he wants to make you happy," Adriana said, still hopeful.

Dromio, misunderstanding her concern, joked, "Oh, he's mad alright, but not in the way you think."

"Mad? What do you mean?" Adriana was taken aback.

"I don't mean he's unfaithful, but he's definitely lost his senses," Dromio clarified. "When I asked him to come home for dinner, all he could talk about was gold. 'It's time to eat,' I said, and all he replied was 'My gold!' over and over. Even when I mentioned you, all he cared about was his gold."

Dromio of Ephesus, looking quite troubled, shared more about his odd encounter with his master. "He claimed he knew nothing of a house, wife, or mistress. So, I ended up carrying his harsh words and a beating back home instead of him," Dromio explained, rubbing his shoulders where he had felt the brunt of his master's frustration.

Adriana, growing impatient, demanded, "Go back and bring him home, you! He needs to be here."

Dromio, almost in disbelief at the thought of facing his master's wrath again, protested, "Should I go back just to be beaten again? Maybe someone else could try their luck?"

Adriana was firm, "Get going, or I might just give you a taste of his temper myself!"

Dromio, trying to lighten the moment with a joke despite his dread, replied, "It seems I'm caught between a rock and a hard place with you two. I'll end up with a head blessed by both your beatings."

Ignoring his pleas, Adriana sent him away, "Enough with your words! Bring back my husband."

Dromio couldn't help but feel like a pawn in a game, "It's like I'm a football, kicked back and forth between you two. If I keep up with this, I'll need to be wrapped in leather for protection!"

As Dromio left to carry out his daunting task, Luciana observed, "Your impatience is showing, sister. It's not helping the situation."

Adriana, feeling ignored and unloved, lamented, "He enjoys the company of others while I'm left wanting for just a smile. Has my beauty faded? Are my conversations no longer interesting? If he finds joy in new clothes, it's not my doing. I cannot control what he does."

Luciana tried to calm her, "Don't let jealousy consume you. It's harmful."

But Adriana couldn't help feeling hurt, "Only those who've never felt such pain can dismiss it so easily. I suspect his affections are elsewhere. Didn't he promise me a chain? If only his promises held as much weight as that chain, perhaps things would be different."

Luciana, seeing her sister's pain, reminded her, "Jealousy is a tricky foe, ensnaring too many in its grasp."

As they exited, the air was heavy with Adriana's sorrow and the complexity of their situation, a reminder of the challenges of love and expectation.

# SCENE 2

In a busy part of town, Antipholus of Syracuse was reflecting on his day. He had given some gold to his servant, Dromio of Syracuse, to keep safe at the Centaur inn. Since then, he hadn't seen Dromio and was wondering where he might be. Just then, Dromio appeared.

"Hey there! Why the long face? You used to find everything funny," Antipholus greeted him, a bit puzzled. "Don't tell me you've forgotten about the Centaur, or the gold, or that my wife wanted us home for dinner? Did you think our house moved to the Phoenix? Were you joking with me earlier?"

Dromio, completely confused, replied, "What are you talking about, sir? I haven't seen you since you sent me to the Centaur with your gold."

Antipholus was surprised and a bit annoyed, "You're saying you didn't get the gold? And what's this about a wife and dinner? I hope you realized I wasn't pleased with those answers."

Dromio, trying to lighten the mood, said, "It's good to see you joking around, but I don't understand this game. What's the punchline?"

Antipholus, not in the mood for jokes, snapped back, "You think I'm joking? This is no laughing matter!" And with that, he gave Dromio a couple of quick taps to emphasize his point.

"Ow! Sir, why are you hitting me? I thought you were joking!" Dromio exclaimed, trying to dodge the blows.

Antipholus explained, "Just because we sometimes joke around doesn't mean you can take liberties. There's a time for fun and a time to be serious. If you can't match your mood to mine, you'll learn the hard way."

Dromio of Syracuse was rubbing his head, feeling a bit sore from the unexpected lesson. "So, you call it a 'sconce'? I'd rather you left my head alone. If this keeps up, I'll need to protect my head, or my brains will slide into my shoulders. But, why am I being hit, sir?"

"Do you really not know?" Antipholus of Syracuse asked, a bit surprised by the question.

"I only know that I've been hit," Dromio replied, still puzzled.

"Want to know the reason?" Antipholus offered.

"Yes, please. They say there's a reason for everything," Dromio said, hoping for some clarity.

"Well, first for mocking me, and then for bringing it up again," Antipholus explained.

Dromio, trying to find some logic in his situation, mused, "Is there ever a right time to be beaten, when the reasons make no sense? Anyway, thank you, sir."

"Thank me? For what?" Antipholus was curious.

"For giving me a bit of something when I wasn't expecting anything," Dromio joked, trying to lighten the mood.

"I guess next time, I'll have to balance it out by giving you nothing when you expect something. But, tell me, is it time for lunch?" Antipholus changed the subject.

"No, sir, I think we're missing something for the meal," Dromio said, hinting at his earlier ordeal.

"And what might that be?" Antipholus asked, intrigued.

"A good basting," Dromio quipped, referring to both cooking and the beating he'd just received.

"Well, if it's dry, I suppose I won't eat it," Antipholus played along.

"I'd recommend you don't, sir, unless you want to end up in a bad mood and give me another 'dry basting'," Dromio said, wrapping up their exchange with a bit of humor to soften the blows.

Antipholus of Syracuse, still in a teaching mood, said, "Remember, there's a right time for jokes. Everything has its moment."

"I would have disagreed with you before you got so quick-tempered," Dromio of Syracuse replied, a little wary now.

"And on what grounds would you argue that?" Antipholus asked, curious about Dromio's logic.

"Well, it's as clear as the bald head of Father Time himself," Dromio started, ready to share his wisdom.

"Go on, I'm listening," Antipholus encouraged him.

Dromio explained, "You can't make hair grow back on a head that's gone bald naturally."

"But can't he fix it with some kind of trick?" Antipholus played along.

"Sure, if by trick you mean buying a wig to cover up someone else's lost hair," Dromio quipped.

"Why do you think Time is so stingy with hair, even though it grows so freely?" Antipholus wondered aloud.

Dromio had a theory, "Time gives animals plenty of hair as a blessing. Maybe he figured humans needed less hair and more brains."

"But some folks have a lot of hair and not much upstairs," Antipholus pointed out.

"Every one of those men had enough sense to lose their hair, one way or another," Dromio countered.

"So, you're saying men with lots of hair are straightforward but not too bright?" Antipholus tried to summarize.

"Exactly. The more straightforward they are, the quicker they lose it, though usually in good spirits," Dromio concluded.

"For what reason would that be?" Antipholus was intrigued.

"For two good reasons," Dromio claimed.

"But they're not solid reasons, are they?" Antipholus challenged.

"Well, if not solid, then they're at least reliable," Dromio assured him, keeping up with the banter despite the earlier tension.

After their playful banter about hair and time, Dromio of Syracuse finally gave Antipholus two "solid" reasons for a man to be happy about losing his hair: to save money on haircuts and to avoid getting hair in his soup. Antipholus joked that their entire conversation proved there's no right time for everything, especially not for regrowing hair lost to nature.

Dromio cleverly added, "Well, since Time himself is bald, those who follow him till the end of the world will likely be bald too."

Antipholus acknowledged the conclusion with a pun, "I knew it would be a 'bald' one."

Their conversation was interrupted by the arrival of Adriana and Luciana. Adriana, looking upset, confronted Antipholus, whom she mistook for her husband, "You look at me as if I'm a stranger. Has another woman captured your heart? There was a time when nothing pleased you unless it came from me. What's changed? Why do you act as if you don't know me?"

She continued, pouring out her feelings of betrayal and fear of being replaced, "Would it hurt you to hear rumors of me being unfaithful, just as it hurts me to think of you turning away from our love? If you found me disloyal, you'd surely cast me aside. Remember, if you're unfaithful, it's as if I share in your mistakes because we are one. So, please stay true to our marriage, to keep us both honorable."

Antipholus of Syracuse was taken aback by Adriana's emotional appeal. "You're speaking to me as if we know each other, but I assure you, I've only been in Ephesus for two hours. I'm as new to your city as I am to this conversation. I'm trying to follow along, but I can't seem to understand a single word."

Luciana, surprised by his response, said, "What's happened to you? You never treated my sister like this before. She asked Dromio to bring you home for dinner."

Antipholus, puzzled, asked, "Dromio?"

Dromio of Syracuse, equally confused, echoed, "Me?"

Adriana insisted, "Yes, you. And you came back saying he hit you and denied knowing me or this house."

Antipholus turned to his servant, "Did you talk to this lady? What agreement do you have with her?"

Dromio was adamant, "Sir, I swear I've never met her until now."

But Antipholus accused him, "That's a lie. You've relayed her words to me yourself."

Dromio remained firm, "I've never spoken to her in my life."

Antipholus then wondered aloud, "How does she know our names if we haven't met? This must be some sort of mistake."

Adriana was frustrated, "It's beneath you to play such games, pretending not to know me, and encouraging your servant to deny our marriage."

She continued, metaphorically describing their relationship, "You're like a strong elm tree, and I'm like a vine that grows around you, drawing strength from you. If anything takes you away from me, it's worthless—like unwanted plants that need to be removed."

Antipholus found himself moved by her words, yet confused, "Is she speaking to me? Was I married to her in a dream? Am I dreaming now? This situation is so strange. But until I understand what's happening, I'll go along with it."

Caught in a web of mistaken identity, Antipholus of Syracuse decides to play along, trying to untangle the truth from the confusion surrounding him and the people of Ephesus.

Luciana, growing impatient with the confusion, directed Dromio, "Dromio, go tell the servants to get dinner ready."

Dromio, feeling quite out of place, muttered to himself, "I must be in a land of magic. Talking with creatures of the night! If we don't follow their commands, who knows what they'll do to us?"

Luciana, annoyed at his mumbling, scolded, "Why are you talking to yourself instead of doing as you're told? Hurry up, you slowpoke!"

Dromio, feeling bewildered, asked, "Master, do I look different to you? I feel like I've been turned into something else."

Antipholus, also feeling out of sorts, replied, "In your mind, maybe, and I feel the same."

"No, I mean really. I feel like I've changed in body too," Dromio insisted.

"You look the same to me," Antipholus assured him.

"But I feel like an ape," Dromio exclaimed.

Luciana chimed in, "If you've turned into anything, it's a donkey."

"That must be it," Dromio agreed, playing along with the metaphor. "I must be a donkey, or I'd recognize her as she recognizes me."

Adriana, tired of the nonsense, decided to take charge. "Enough of this foolishness. I won't stand here and cry over your jokes. Let's go to dinner. Dromio, you stay and guard the door. My husband and I will dine upstairs today, and I'll deal with your mischief later. If anyone asks for you, say you're not available. Make sure no one else comes in."

Antipholus, still perplexed by the situation, wondered aloud, "Am I on Earth or somewhere else? Is this a dream? How can it be that I don't recognize myself, and yet I'm supposed to play along with this farce?"

Dromio, wanting to be sure of his duties, asked, "So, I'm to guard the door, then?"

"Yes, and make sure you do it well, or you'll answer to me," Adriana warned.

Luciana urged them, "Let's not delay any longer. It's time to eat."

And with that, they all went their separate ways, leaving Antipholus and Dromio to navigate through their bewildering circumstances in Ephesus, unsure of what was real and what was not.

# ACT III

# SCENE 1

In front of Antipholus of Ephesus's house, Antipholus, his servant Dromio of Ephesus, Angelo, and Balthazar were having a conversation.

Antipholus of Ephesus explained to Angelo, "Please forgive us for any trouble. My wife gets upset if I'm late. Just say I was with you at your shop looking at the necklace you're making for her, and you'll deliver it tomorrow. But this guy," he pointed at Dromio of Ephesus, "claims I met him in the market, beat him, and then refused to acknowledge my own wife and home."

Dromio of Ephesus defended himself, "You can say whatever you want, but I know what happened. You did beat me, and if my bruises could write, they'd spell out exactly what I think of you."

Antipholus, frustrated, retorted, "I think you're nothing but a fool."

Dromio cleverly replied, "Well, that seems about right, considering how I've been treated. If I'm a fool for getting kicked, I ought to kick back, unless you're afraid of getting kicked by a 'fool'."

Trying to lighten the mood, Antipholus turned to Balthazar, "You seem a bit down, Balthazar. I hope our hospitality can match our intentions and your good company."

Balthazar, ever polite, responded, "Your food may not be extravagant, sir, but your welcome is very much appreciated."

Antipholus joked about the offerings, "Whether it's meat or fish, a warm welcome is the best ingredient for any meal."

Balthazar pointed out, "Good food is easy to come by; it's the warmth of the welcome that makes a meal special."

Antipholus agreed, "True, a warm welcome is just words, but they can mean a lot."

Balthazar said, "Even a simple meal can be a feast with a hearty welcome."

Antipholus, was already feeling quite hungry and looking forward to the meal. "Ah, I may not have the fanciest food to offer," he mused aloud, "but I serve it with all my heart. Oh, wait, why is my door locked? Dromio, go ask them to let us in."

Dromio of Ephesus, his servant, called out to the maids, "Maud, Bridget, Marian, Cicely, Gillian, Ginn! Someone open the door!"

But then, from inside, Dromio of Syracuse's voice could be heard mocking, "Calling for so many when one is too many? Move away from the door!"

Confused, Dromio of Ephesus wondered aloud, "Who's taken over the door? My master can't wait outside!"

"To him then," retorted Dromio of Syracuse from inside. "Let him go back where he came from before he gets cold feet."

Antipholus, growing impatient, demanded, "Who's speaking? Open up! I'm here for my dinner; I haven't eaten all day."

"You won't eat here today," came Dromio of Syracuse's cheeky reply. "Come back another day."

Antipholus, now irritated, asked, "Who dares keep me from entering my own house?"

"It's Dromio, the porter for now," came the answer from within.

Dromio of Ephesus felt insulted. "Oh, you thief! Stealing both my job and name. If you were me today, you'd wish you were anyone but yourself."

Inside, Luce, another servant, puzzled by the noise, asked, "What's happening, Dromio? Who's at the door?"

"Just let my master in, Luce," pleaded Dromio of Ephesus, hoping to finally get Antipholus inside for his much-awaited meal.

Luce, still inside, playfully refused to open the door, "Nope, you're too late for that. Tell your master that."

Dromio of Ephesus couldn't help but laugh at the situation. "Oh, I've got a joke for you. Ready to hear it?"

Luce responded with her own tease, "Sure, but when will you ever get it right?"

From inside, Dromio of Syracuse cheered Luce on, "Well said, Luce!"

Antipholus of Ephesus, growing more impatient by the minute, pleaded, "Hey! You're going to let us in, right?"

Luce cheekily replied, "I was about to ask you the same thing."

"And you wouldn't let us in," added Dromio of Syracuse from inside.

Dromio of Ephesus joined in the playful banter, "Nice exchange there! It's like we're trading punches."

Antipholus, trying to be stern, demanded, "Open up, you troublesome servant!"

Luce, still not budging, teased, "Whose sake should I open the door for, I wonder?"

Antipholus, frustrated, urged his servant, "Dromio, bang on that door harder!"

Luce remained unmoved, "He can knock all he wants. It won't change my mind."

Antipholus threatened, "You'll regret this if I have to break this door down."

"Why all this fuss?" Luce retorted. "Isn't there a place for troublemakers like you?"

Suddenly, Adriana, hearing the commotion, asked, "Who's making all this noise at the door?"

Dromio of Syracuse quipped, "It seems your town is full of mischievous boys."

Antipholus, realizing his wife was also inside, called out, "Are you there, my dear? You could have let me in sooner."

Adriana, feigning ignorance, replied, "Your wife? Please, you've got the wrong house."

Dromio of Ephesus humorously added, "Oh, if only pain could enter, you'd be the first through the door."

Angelo, who had been quietly observing, noted, "There's neither a warm welcome nor a friendly face here. We were hoping for at least one of those."

Luce, still inside, playfully refused to let them in, "No, he's too late for that, and that's what you can tell your master."

Dromio of Ephesus couldn't help but laugh, trying to match her wit, "Shall I come in with a joke then?"

Luce shot back, "Sure, if you can figure out when."

From inside, Dromio of Syracuse cheered Luce on, "Well said, Luce!"

Antipholus of Ephesus, growing more impatient, pleaded, "You're going to let us in, right?"

"I was about to ask you the same," Luce teased.

Dromio of Syracuse joined in, "But you already got your answer, no."

Dromio of Ephesus joked, "Ah, a good hit! That was like a tit for tat."

Antipholus of Ephesus then demanded, "Let me in, you troublemaker!"

"For whom?" Luce teased further.

"Master, let's knock harder," suggested Dromio of Ephesus.

"Keep knocking if you enjoy it," Luce retorted.

Antipholus warned, "You'll regret this if I have to break down the door."

"Why all this fuss when there's a simpler solution?" Luce replied smartly.

Adriana, curious about the commotion, asked from inside, "Who's making all this noise at the door?"

Dromio of Syracuse quipped, "Ah, your town has too many unruly kids."

Antipholus, recognizing his wife's voice, called out, "Why didn't you come sooner?"

"Your wife? I'm no doorkeeper. Go away," Adriana responded sharply.

Dromio of Ephesus humorously added, "If pain made one leave, this 'doorkeeper' would surely go."

Angelo, observing the standoff, noted, "We're neither welcomed nor entertained. We hoped for either."

Balthazar, trying to mediate, suggested, "By arguing over it, we end up with neither."

Dromio of Ephesus encouraged, "They're waiting, master. Let's welcome them."

Antipholus sensed something amiss, "Something's blocking our way in."

Dromio of Ephesus agreed, "You'd feel it more if you were cold. It's frustrating to be locked out."

Antipholus, determined, said, "I'll find a way in. Fetch me a tool."

Dromio of Syracuse warned from inside, "Try breaking in and see what happens!"

Dromio of Ephesus mused, "Words are just air, but some might land squarely."

Dromio of Syracuse taunted back, "Seems you need a lesson too!"

Dromio of Ephesus, tired of the back and forth, pleaded, "Enough! Let me in."

"To that," Dromio of Syracuse joked, "when pigs fly!"

Antipholus then decided, "I'll force my way in. Get me a crowbar."

Dromio of Ephesus quipped, "A crow? As in the bird without feathers?"

Balthazar, seeing the escalating tension, advised patience. "Consider your reputation and your wife's honor. Maybe there's a reason for this. Let's eat elsewhere and return later to understand this mystery. Acting rashly now could harm your good name forever."

Antipholus of Ephesus, finally agreeing to the advice given, declared, "Alright, you've convinced me. I'll leave without causing a scene. Despite the oddness of the day, I plan to enjoy myself. I know a lady who is charming and clever, both lively and kind. We'll have our meal with her. This lady, my wife, has often criticized me without reason. But today, we will dine at her table."

Turning to Angelo, he instructed, "Go home and bring the chain that's been made for me. Take it to the Porpentine; that's where we'll be. I'll give the chain to the hostess there, partly to annoy my wife. Hurry, please. Since my own home won't welcome me, I'll see if I'm welcome elsewhere."

Angelo agreed, "I'll meet you there in a while."

Antipholus of Ephesus nodded, "Do that. This prank will likely cost me, but it's worth the fun." And with that, they all went their separate ways, each to prepare for the next part of the day's adventure.

# SCENE 2

Luciana approached Antipholus of Syracuse, concerned and puzzled. "Have you forgotten how to be a loving husband?" she asked. "Why does your love seem to wither just as it's beginning to bloom? If you married my sister for her wealth, at least treat her kindly for that. If your heart lies elsewhere, hide your unfaithfulness; don't let her see it in your eyes or hear it in your words. Pretend to be loyal, even if you're not. It's cruel to make her suspect your love for her is gone."

Antipholus of Syracuse, confused by her words, replied, "I don't know who you think I am, but your words are as puzzling as they are beautiful. You ask me to pretend and hide, but why should I live a lie? I don't understand what you're trying to say. Are you trying to change me, make me someone I'm not?"

He continued, clearly lost, "If I'm the person you think I am, then I must tell you, your sister is not my wife. I don't owe her any loyalty. In fact, I feel a stronger connection to you. Don't try to win me over with sweet words, only to drown me in sorrow. If you must sing, sing for yourself, and I'll be captivated by you alone. Let's not pretend; let's be honest with each other."

Luciana was puzzled by Antipholus's words. "Are you out of your mind to talk like this?"

Antipholus of Syracuse, feeling trapped in a confusing situation, replied, "I'm not mad, just completely baffled."

"It's your eyes that are causing this trouble," Luciana pointed out.

"It's because I've been dazzled by your beauty," he admitted.

"Look where you're supposed to, and you'll see clearly," she advised.

"To me, that's like closing my eyes to the beauty of the night when I'm with you," he responded.

"Why do you call me 'love'? You should call my sister that," Luciana insisted.

"You are like a sister to me," Antipholus tried to explain.

"That would be my sister," Luciana corrected him.

"No, it's you. You're the other half of me, the best part of me," Antipholus confessed, expressing his unexpected feelings for Luciana. "You're everything I could hope for."

"But all those things you said should be true for my sister," Luciana reminded him.

Antipholus, however, saw it differently. "But it's you I feel this connection with, not her. I see a future with you, not as siblings, but something more."

Luciana, unsure what to do, said, "Wait here. I'll go get my sister; we need her blessing."

After she left, Dromio of Syracuse rushed in, prompting Antipholus to ask, "Dromio, why are you running like that?"

"Do you recognize me? Am I Dromio? Am I your servant? Am I even myself?" Dromio questioned, caught up in his own confusion.

"Yes, you're Dromio, you're my servant, and you're definitely yourself," Antipholus reassured him, even as they both navigated their strange circumstances.

Dromio of Syracuse, feeling overwhelmed, exclaimed, "I'm in a real pickle, sir. I seem to be claimed by a woman, followed around by her, and she insists that I belong to her."

Antipholus of Syracuse was curious, "What woman claims you, and why do you feel so troubled by this?"

"Well, sir, she claims me like someone might claim a horse they own. She wants me around, but it's more like she sees me as an animal. And she's quite a character, one you'd hesitate to talk about without being respectful," Dromio explained.

"And who is she?" Antipholus asked.

"She's someone you'd have to speak of with respect, but let's just say, I didn't get lucky in this match. She's quite... substantial," Dromio said delicately.

"What do you mean by 'substantial'?" pressed Antipholus.

"Let's just say she's the kitchen maid, very much accustomed to grease. I can't think of any use for her, except maybe as a lamp to light the way, given how much she could burn," Dromio joked.

"And what does she look like?" Antipholus inquired, going along with the banter.

"Dark-skinned, sir, and not exactly clean. You could slip on the floor just from the grease she's covered in," Dromio described with a hint of humor.

"But couldn't that be washed off?" Antipholus suggested.

"No, sir, it's deep-rooted. Not even a flood could clean her," Dromio quipped.

"And what's her name?" Antipholus finally asked.

"Her name's Nell, sir. But joke aside, she's so wide, I reckon you'd need more than a yardstick to measure her width," Dromio concluded, trying to lighten the mood with a bit of humor amidst their confusing day.

Antipholus of Syracuse, amused by Dromio's description, played along. "So, she's quite large?"

"Yes, she's round like a globe. I could map out countries on her," Dromio of Syracuse joked.

"And where would Ireland be on this globe?" Antipholus asked, joining in the jest.

"In her behind, sir. I figured it out by the bogs," Dromio replied, keeping up with the humor.

"And Scotland?" Antipholus inquired, entertained by the game.

"By the roughness of her hands, sir, as barren as Scotland's lands," Dromio described.

"What about France?" continued Antipholus.

"On her forehead, sir, always in opposition, like France against its ruler," Dromio said cleverly.

"And England?" asked Antipholus.

"I couldn't find the white cliffs, but perhaps in her chin, with the salty tears running between it and France," Dromio quipped.

"Where did you find Spain?" Antipholus wanted to know.

"In her hot breath, sir, I didn't see it, but I sure felt it," Dromio responded.

"And the far-off lands of America, the Indies?" asked Antipholus, enjoying the geography lesson.

"All over her nose, sir, adorned with jewels as if they were treasures from the New World, heated by Spain's breath," Dromio elaborated.

"And what about the Netherlands, Belgia?" Antipholus asked, curious about the next location.

"I didn't venture that far down, sir," Dromio said, concluding their whimsical journey. "In the end, this woman, claiming to be a soothsayer, called me Dromio, claimed I was betrothed to her, and even knew of marks on my body, convincing me she was some kind of witch. Had I not been steadfast in faith and courage, she might have turned me into a little dog, doomed to run in circles."

Antipholus of Syracuse, feeling overwhelmed by the peculiar events of the day, made a quick decision. "Hurry to the port, Dromio. If there's any chance to leave this town by sea, I'll take it. I won't stay here tonight. Meet me at the marketplace if a ship is leaving. It's strange that everyone knows us, yet we know nobody. It's time to leave."

Dromio of Syracuse, equally eager to escape his own bizarre predicament, agreed, "Just as one would run from a bear, I'll run from the woman who claims to be my wife." And with that, he left to follow Antipholus's instructions.

Alone, Antipholus reflected on his situation, "This place must be filled with witches, for such strange things to happen. The woman who calls me husband is someone I cannot bear, but her sister, with her grace and charm, almost makes me forget myself. Yet, I must resist her like one would avoid a siren's song."

Just then, Angelo approached, bearing the gold chain. "Master Antipholus," he greeted.

"Yes, that's me," Antipholus replied, puzzled.

"I've brought the chain you ordered. I was delayed because it wasn't finished. I assumed I would find you at the Porpentine," Angelo explained, handing over the chain.

Antipholus was confused, "What am I to do with this? I didn't order it."

Angelo insisted, "You've asked for it many times. Take it home, please your wife with it. I'll come by at supper to collect my payment."

Antipholus, trying to resolve the confusion, suggested, "Take the payment now, in case you never see me or the chain again."

Angelo laughed it off, "You're quite the joker. Farewell."

As Angelo left, Antipholus mused, "I don't know what to make of this. But who would refuse such a beautiful gift? It seems one doesn't need to work hard for wealth in this city if such gifts are freely given. I'll wait at the marketplace for Dromio and take the first chance to leave by ship."

He quickly headed to the mart, pondering the day's surreal encounters and the unexpected gift, ready to leave the city at the first opportunity.

# ACT IV

# SCENE 1

In a busy square, Second Merchant, Angelo, and an officer were having a serious conversation. Second Merchant was getting impatient, "Since Pentecost, you've owed me money, Angelo. I wouldn't bother you now if I didn't need to go to Persia. I need that money for my trip. Pay up, or I'll have this officer take action."

Angelo tried to explain his situation calmly, "The exact amount I owe you is supposed to come from Antipholus. He just took a chain from me, and by five, I'm supposed to get paid for it. If you don't mind, let's go to his house together. I'll settle my debt with you."

Just then, Antipholus of Ephesus and his servant Dromio walked up from the direction of the courtesan's house. The officer pointed them out, "Look, there's no need to wait. Here comes Antipholus himself."

Antipholus of Ephesus seemed preoccupied with his own problems, barely noticing them at first. "Dromio, while I deal with the goldsmith, you go buy a rope. I plan to use it on my wife and her friends for locking me out today. Oh, but wait, there's Angelo. Forget the rope for now; we'll talk to him."

Dromio, confused but obedient, quipped, "I guess I'm buying a rope then," before hurrying off on his errand.

Turning his attention to Angelo, Antipholus of Ephesus couldn't hide his irritation, "I was expecting you and that chain at my house, but you never showed. Did you think our friendship would break like a weak chain?"

Angelo, trying to lighten the mood, responded, "I didn't forget you. Here's the bill for the chain, showing its weight and the gold's quality. It's a bit more than what I owe the Second Merchant here. Could you please settle this so he can be on his way? He's in a rush to catch a ship."

Antipholus of Ephesus, caught off guard, responded, "I don't have the money on me right now, and I have things to do in town. Why don't you take the chain to my house? Ask my wife to pay you. I might even meet you there."

Angelo, looking for clarification, asked, "So, you'll bring the chain to her yourself?"

"No, take it with you, just in case I'm delayed," Antipholus replied, wanting to ensure Angelo wasn't left waiting.

"Alright, but do you have the chain with you now?" Angelo inquired, trying to sort out the confusion.

"If I don't, I hope you do," Antipholus said, hinting Angelo might be responsible for the chain at the moment. "Otherwise, you won't get your money."

Angelo, growing impatient, pressed him, "Please, let's not delay any further. The chain, if you have it, hand it over. This gentleman has been waiting too long because of me."

Antipholus, frustrated, accused Angelo of using the situation as an excuse for not keeping his promise. "You're turning this into a bigger issue than it is. Shouldn't you have brought the chain to me earlier?"

The Second Merchant, aware of the time passing, urged them to hurry. "Please, let's conclude this. Do you have an answer for me, or should I leave this to the officer?"

Angelo, stuck in the middle, appealed again for the chain or some sign of payment from Antipholus.

Antipholus, increasingly exasperated, demanded, "Stop joking around. Where's the chain? Show it to me."

With everyone growing more impatient, the situation threatened to escalate, hinging on the mysterious whereabouts of the chain and the unresolved payment.

Antipholus of Ephesus expressed his frustration, "Why should I answer you? I don't owe you until I have the chain."

Angelo insisted, "But I gave you the chain half an hour ago."

Antipholus denied receiving anything, "You didn't give me anything. You're accusing me wrongly."

Angelo, feeling his honor at stake, retorted, "It's you who wrong me by denying it. My reputation is on the line here."

At this point, the Second Merchant had enough and instructed the officer to arrest Antipholus. The officer, following orders, declared Antipholus under arrest in the duke's name, compelling him to comply.

Angelo, seeking to preserve his credit, pressed for payment, "This is about my reputation. You must pay, or I'll have the officer detain you."

Antipholus, defiant, challenged Angelo, "You expect me to pay for something I never received? Arrest me if you dare."

Angelo, determined to uphold his claim, paid the officer to arrest Antipholus, emphasizing the seriousness of his accusation, "I'd do the same even if he were my brother who insulted me like this."

The officer then formally arrested Antipholus, who warned that Angelo would pay dearly for this misunderstanding.

Angelo, undeterred, stood firm on seeking justice, confident in his position.

In the midst of this escalating conflict, Dromio of Syracuse arrived with news of a ship ready to leave, unaware of the turmoil his master was in. He reported everything was ready for their departure, awaiting only Antipholus's arrival.

Antipholus of Ephesus, caught in a whirlwind of confusion and frustration, mistook Dromio of Syracuse for his own servant. "What madness is this? What ship from Epidamnum waits for me?"

Dromio of Syracuse, equally confused, tried to explain, "It's the ship you told me to find, for our journey."

Antipholus, thinking he had asked for something entirely different, scolded him, "You fool, I asked for a rope, not a ship. You're mixing things up."

Dromio, steadfast in his understanding, insisted, "But sir, you did ask me to find a ship at the bay."

Realizing the argument was going nowhere, Antipholus decided to focus on his immediate problem. "We'll sort this out later. For now, go to Adriana, give her this key, and tell her to send the purse of ducats from the desk covered in Turkish tapestry. It's to bail me out. Hurry up and go!"

As Antipholus was taken away by the officer, Dromio of Syracuse lamented his predicament. "Back to Adriana's, where that woman claimed me as her husband? She's a bit too much for me to handle. But I must go, even if unwillingly. A servant has to do as they're told."

And with that, Dromio hurried off to fulfill Antipholus's request, hoping to resolve the chaotic situation, while pondering the strange turn of events that had led him to be mistaken for someone else's husband.

# SCENE 2

Adriana, worried and confused, sought Luciana's insights about her earlier encounter with Antipholus. "Luciana, how did he behave towards you? Could you tell if he was serious or not by looking into his eyes? Was he joyful or sad, pale or flushed?"

Luciana shared her observations, "He first claimed that you had no claim over him."

Adriana interpreted this bitterly, "Meaning he owes me nothing, which only adds to my frustration."

Luciana continued, "He then insisted he was a stranger in this place."

"A truth he swore, though he was indeed lying," Adriana noted, recognizing the irony in his words.

"I argued on your behalf," Luciana added.

"And what was his response?" Adriana pressed.

"He claimed the love I was asking for you, he was asking from me," Luciana revealed.

Curious, Adriana inquired, "How did he try to win you over?"

"With words that could sway any honest heart. He complimented my looks and then my way of speaking," Luciana recounted.

Adriana, struggling with her feelings, declared, "I can't and won't stay silent. My heart may hold him dear, but my words will not. He's flawed in every way, in appearance, in behavior—everywhere lacking."

Luciana reasoned, "Who would be jealous of such a man? When bad is gone, it's not missed."

But Adriana reflected deeper, "Yet, in my eyes, he's more than what my words can paint. I wish others saw less in him. Though I curse him with my words, my heart is with him."

In the midst of their heartfelt discussion, Dromio of Syracuse burst in, gasping for air from his run. "Quick, the desk, the purse! Hurry!"

Luciana, seeing his distress, asked, "Why are you so out of breath?"

"From running fast," Dromio panted, delivering his urgent message.

Adriana, concerned for her husband, quickly asked Dromio of Syracuse, "Where is your master? Is he okay?"

Dromio, with a flair for the dramatic, replied, "No, he's caught in a dreadful place, worse than hell itself. A devil in a uniform has him, with a heart as hard as steel."

Adriana, puzzled and worried, pressed, "What are you talking about?"

"I'm not entirely sure, but he's been arrested," Dromio explained, using his wit to describe the situation.

"Arrested? By whom?" Adriana urgently inquired.

"I'm not sure who's behind it, but he's wrapped up in trouble—that much I know. Can we send him some money for bail?" Dromio suggested, hinting at the solution.

"Go get it," Adriana instructed Luciana, who quickly left to fetch the purse.

Adriana then pondered, "It's strange that he would owe money without my knowledge. Was he arrested because of a debt?"

"Not because of a debt, but something more tangible—a chain," Dromio quipped, playing with his words.

"A chain?" Adriana was confused.

Dromio, ever the joker, replied, "No, I mean the bell signals it's time for me to go. It was two when I left him, and now it's somehow one."

Adriana, amused despite the situation, commented on the absurdity of time running backward.

Dromio continued his jest, "Time's a tricky thing, always running out or stealing away. Maybe that's why it seemed to go backward when faced with trouble."

As Luciana returned with the purse, Adriana handed it to Dromio, "Take this to him quickly and bring him back."

As they prepared to leave, Adriana thought of her mixed feelings—her worries and the strange turns of the day weighing heavily on her mind.

# SCENE 3

Antipholus of Syracuse was feeling quite bewildered as he walked through the town. "Every person I pass greets me like an old friend, knows my name, and acts overly familiar. Some even offer me money or goods as if I owed them. It's as if this place is full of magic or trickery," he mused, puzzled by the day's strange encounters.

Just then, Dromio of Syracuse arrived, out of breath from running. "Master, I've brought the gold you asked for. Did you manage to get a new outfit from that guy, Adam, the one who's always locking people up?"

Antipholus, confused by Dromio's words, asked, "What gold? And what do you mean by Adam?"

Dromio explained, "Not the biblical Adam, but the jailer named Adam, the one who dresses in leather and follows you around, suggesting you should give up your freedom."

Antipholus was still confused. "I don't follow your meaning."

Dromio tried to clarify, "I'm talking about the officer, the one who carries a leather baton and arrests people, making them wear prison clothes. He's like a bad omen, always suggesting it's time to rest—in jail."

Finally understanding, Antipholus realized Dromio was referring to an officer of the law. "Oh, you mean the sergeant, the one who enforces the law and makes people pay for breaking their promises?"

"Yes, exactly," Dromio confirmed, "the one who's all too eager to put people to bed early, in jail, with his favorite phrase, 'God give you good rest!'"

Antipholus of Syracuse, feeling overwhelmed by the confusing events of the day, tried to make sense of it all. "Let's just focus on getting through this," he said, hoping for some clarity amidst the chaos.

Dromio handed him some coins, "Here's the money you asked for, to help us out of this situation."

Just then, a lady approached, greeting Antipholus cheerfully and inquiring about a chain he had supposedly promised her earlier. This unexpected encounter only added to his bewilderment. "Stay away! Don't come any closer," Antipholus pleaded, mistaking her intentions.

Dromio, trying to understand but only adding to the confusion, asked, "Is this lady someone bad?"

Antipholus, caught up in the moment, replied, "It feels like she's causing us trouble."

The lady, amused by their banter, suggested they join her for a meal to lighten the mood.

Dromio, seizing the opportunity for a joke, warned his master, "If you dine with her, make sure to use a long spoon."

Puzzled, Antipholus asked, "And why's that?"

"Because it's said you need a long spoon to dine safely with tricky characters," Dromio explained, trying to make light of the situation.

Antipholus, having had enough of the day's strange encounters, firmly declined the lady's invitation. "I think we should keep our distance. We've had enough surprises for one day."

The lady approached Antipholus, her voice laced with a hint of impatience, "Please return the ring you held onto during dinner, or, as a trade, the chain you promised me. Then, I'll leave you in peace, sir."

Dromio of Syracuse, always quick to add his own twist, chimed in, "Some troublesome spirits are satisfied with mere trifles—a bit of nail, a strand of hair, or even a cherry stone. But this lady here demands a chain. Master, think carefully before you act. If you hand it over, we might end up being haunted by more than just demands."

The lady persisted, her request clear, "I kindly ask for either my ring or the chain you promised. I trust you're not planning to deceive me."

Antipholus of Syracuse, feeling cornered and confused, replied sharply, "Stay away, you troublemaker! Come on, Dromio, let's leave this place."

Dromio of Syracuse couldn't resist adding a witty remark as they hurried away, "'Pride goes before a fall,' as the peacock says. You know that well, madam."

Left alone, the lady could only conclude that Antipholus must be out of his mind to behave so erratically. "He must be mad, or he wouldn't have acted so disgracefully. He has a ring of mine worth a good sum, and he promised me a chain in exchange, but now he denies me both. His madness seems the only explanation, especially after the wild story he shared at dinner about being locked out of his own home. Perhaps his wife, knowing of his condition, intentionally kept him out. I must go to his house and inform his wife of his lunacy—that he barged into my home and forcefully took my ring. This seems the best course of action, for I cannot afford to lose what is rightfully mine." With her plan set, she departed, determined to seek justice for her loss.

# SCENE 4

Antipholus of Ephesus, accompanied by an officer, reassured him, "Don't worry; I'm not going to run off. I'll pay you enough to cover my bail before we part ways. My wife's not in the best mood today, and she might not trust anyone sent to inform her of my arrest. She'd find the news quite upsetting."

Just then, Dromio of Ephesus appeared, holding a rope. Antipholus, hopeful, asked, "Is that the money I asked you to fetch?"

Dromio, misunderstanding the task, proudly presented the rope, "Here's what you need to settle all debts."

Confused and annoyed, Antipholus pressed, "But where's the money?"

"I spent the money on this rope," Dromio admitted, thinking he had followed his master's instructions.

"Incredulous, Antipholus exclaimed, "You spent five hundred ducats on a rope?"

Dromio, trying to lighten the mood, joked, "Well, I'm here to serve, and I've brought what you asked for at that price."

Frustrated, Antipholus questioned the purpose of his servant's errand, "Why did I send you home in the first place?"

"To fetch a rope's end, sir, and here I am, having completed that task," Dromio responded, missing the gravity of the situation.

Antipholus, unable to contain his anger, began to scold and physically reprimand Dromio, who pleaded for understanding from the officer.

"Please, be patient with me," Dromio implored Antipholus, trying to dodge the blows.

The officer intervened, urging Antipholus to calm down, but Dromio humorously suggested it would be better if the officer could persuade his master to stop hitting him instead.

Amidst the confusion and misunderstanding, Dromio wistfully wished he couldn't feel the punishment being meted out, highlighting the mix-up and its painful consequences for him.

Antipholus of Ephesus, frustrated and feeling misunderstood, retorted to Dromio, "The only thing you're aware of is getting hit, just like a stubborn donkey."

Dromio of Ephesus, accepting the comparison with a touch of humor, replied, "Indeed, I might as well be a donkey, considering how I've been treated. From the day I was born until now, all I've received for my service are beatings. Whether I'm cold or hot, tired or awake, at home or away, I'm greeted with the same harsh welcome."

As they were talking, Adriana, Luciana, the lady, and Doctor Pinch approached them. Dromio, seeing his mistress, tried to warn her with a saying, hinting at the beatings he endured, "Mistress, consider how things will end, or heed the warning about the rope's end."

Antipholus, annoyed by Dromio's continued chatter, didn't hesitate to discipline him again.

The lady then questioned Adriana, "Do you see? Isn't your husband acting irrationally?"

Adriana agreed, seeing Antipholus's unusual behavior as further proof of his troubled state. She turned to Doctor Pinch, hoping he could restore her husband's sanity, "Doctor Pinch, you have the skills of a magician. Please bring him back to his senses, and I'll be forever grateful."

Luciana observed Antipholus's agitated state, while the lady pointed out his physical reaction to his confusion.

Doctor Pinch, attempting to assess Antipholus's condition, asked for his hand to check his pulse. Antipholus, mistaking the gesture for another threat, retaliated.

Doctor Pinch then tried to exorcise what he believed was a demonic possession, appealing to divine intervention to cure Antipholus, "I command the evil spirit inside this man to leave, by the power of all the saints."

Antipholus of Ephesus, trying to assert his sanity amidst the chaos, implored, "Enough of this foolishness, wizard. I'm not mad."

Adriana, distressed by the scene unfolding before her, wished deeply for his words to be true, "Oh, if only you weren't, my poor troubled husband."

Antipholus, his frustration boiling over, turned to Adriana, "Are these the kinds of guests you entertain? Did this lady with the flashy attire enjoy herself at my house today, while I was unjustly kept outside, denied entrance to my own home?"

Adriana, struggling to maintain her composure, insisted, "My dear, God knows you were at home for dinner. How I wish you had stayed there, away from these accusations and this embarrassing spectacle."

Antipholus, incredulous and angry, demanded, "At home for dinner? What nonsense is this?"

Dromio of Ephesus, caught in the middle, truthfully responded, "To be honest, sir, you did not dine at home."

"Wasn't it so that my own doors were locked against me?" Antipholus pursued the truth of the day's events.

"Indeed, sir, your doors were locked, and you were outside," Dromio confirmed.

"And she insulted me right there, did she not?" Antipholus sought validation for his experience.

"Without a doubt, she did insult you," Dromio affirmed.

"Didn't her maid also mock and deride me?" Antipholus pressed on, seeking further confirmation of his mistreatment.

"Yes, she did; the maid scorned you too," Dromio replied, supporting his master's account.

"And in anger, I left that place, didn't I?" Antipholus recounted his reaction to the insults.

"You certainly did, sir. My own aches are proof of your anger since then," Dromio said, referring to the beatings he endured.

Adriana, unsure how to handle the situation, wondered if agreeing with him was wise. Pinch, observing the dynamics, believed that indulging Antipholus might be the best way to manage his apparent delusion.

Antipholus, feeling betrayed, accused Adriana, "You even conspired with the goldsmith to have me arrested."

Adriana, attempting to clarify the situation, expressed her intention, "I sent you money for your release, through Dromio here, who was supposed to fetch it quickly."

Dromio of Ephesus, puzzled, responded, "Money through me? I only brought back goodwill and a message, but not a single coin, master."

Antipholus of Ephesus, increasingly frustrated, questioned Dromio, "Didn't I send you for a purse of ducats to her?"

Adriana confirmed the transaction, "He came to me, and I handed over the money."

Luciana supported her sister, "I was there; I saw her give it to him."

Dromio of Ephesus, still confused, insisted, "All I was sent for was a rope, nothing about any ducats!"

Doctor Pinch, observing the tense situation, concluded, "Both master and servant are under some strange affliction. Their pale looks suggest it might be best to secure them safely away."

Antipholus, feeling wronged and seeking answers, pressed, "Then why was I locked out today? And why deny sending the gold to me?"

Adriana gently protested, "My dear, I never locked you out."

Dromio of Ephesus added to the confusion, "Master, I indeed received no gold; however, it's true we couldn't enter."

Adriana, frustrated by the conflicting stories, accused them of dishonesty, "You're both speaking falsely!"

Antipholus of Ephesus, enraged and feeling betrayed, accused Adriana of treachery, "You're deceiving me in everything! You've sided with others to mock and scorn me."

As the argument heated, bystanders intervened, trying to restrain Antipholus, who resisted, believing himself surrounded by enemies.

Adriana, fearing for her safety, cried out for help, "Bind him, for our protection!"

Doctor Pinch saw this as evidence of demonic influence, "The evil within him is strong. We need more help."

Luciana, witnessing Antipholus's distress, felt sympathy for him, remarking on his ghastly appearance, a sign of the deep misunderstanding that had taken root among them.

Antipholus of Ephesus, feeling cornered and desperate, cried out, "Are you trying to kill me? Officer, I'm your prisoner. Will you let them take me by force?"

The officer, asserting his duty, responded, "Let him be. He's under my charge, and you can't take him."

Doctor Pinch, seeing the chaos, suggested, "Bind this man too; he's lost his senses as well," as they moved to restrain Dromio of Ephesus.

Adriana, distressed by the unfolding events, questioned the officer's intentions, "Do you take pleasure in seeing a man harm himself in his distress?"

The officer explained his position, "He's my responsibility. If I release him, I'll be held accountable for his debts."

Adriana, seeking a resolution, offered a solution, "I'll settle his debts before I leave. Take me to the creditor, and I'll pay what's owed. Doctor, please ensure he's safely taken to my home. What a terribly unfortunate day this has turned out to be!"

Antipholus, lashing out in his frustration, exclaimed, "Oh, what a day of misery!"

Dromio, trying to lighten the mood despite the tension, joked about his loyalty, "I'm in this mess with you, master."

Antipholus, irate and confused, rebuked him, "Curse you, villain! Why do you provoke me?"

Dromio, with a mix of wit and resignation, replied, "Why not embrace the madness, master? Just blame the devil."

Luciana, observing their banter, lamented, "How sadly they speak, lost in their confusion."

Adriana, determined to take action, instructed, "Take him away. Sister, come with me," as they all departed except for Adriana, Luciana, the officer, and the lady.

Adriana, seeking to understand the situation better, asked, "Under whose complaint is he detained?"

The officer revealed, "He's held on a claim by Angelo, the goldsmith. Do you know him?"

Adriana recognized the name, "Yes, I'm familiar with him. How much does my husband owe?"

"Two hundred ducats," the officer informed.

Curious about the debt's origins, Adriana inquired further, "And how did this debt come to be?"

The officer clarified to Adriana, "The debt is for a chain your husband received from him."

Adriana responded, somewhat confused, "He mentioned ordering a chain for me, but I never saw it."

The lady then interjected with her own experience, "Today, your husband, in a fit of rage, came to my place and took my ring—which I noticed he was wearing just now. Right after that, I saw him with a chain."

Adriana, trying to piece everything together, admitted, "That may be true, but I've never seen such a chain. Officer, please take me to the goldsmith. I need to understand the full story."

Suddenly, Antipholus of Syracuse and his servant Dromio appeared, swords drawn, ready to defend themselves against any further misunderstandings or attacks.

Luciana, alarmed at their return, cried out, "Heavens protect us! They've escaped and are armed!"

Adriana, concerned for their safety, suggested, "We need more help to secure them once more."

The officer, sensing the danger, urged everyone to flee, "Let's get out of here, or we might be harmed."

As everyone else left, Antipholus of Syracuse observed, "It seems our swords have scared these so-called witches away."

Dromio of Syracuse made a light-hearted comment, "The lady eager to be your wife just ran off from you."

Antipholus, eager to leave the chaos behind, said, "Let's head back to the Centaur and collect our belongings. I'm eager to leave this place for good."

Dromio, still finding humor in the situation, suggested, "Why not stay the night? They seem to mean no harm; they even offer us gold. Aside from the lady claiming me in marriage, I might have stayed, tempted by the kindness we've found here."

But Antipholus was determined, "I won't stay here another night, not for the entire town. Let's make haste to secure our things for departure."

With that decision made, they exited, intent on leaving Ephesus and its bewildering encounters behind them.

# ACT V

# SCENE 1

At the street before the Priory, Angelo and the Second Merchant engaged in a serious conversation.

Angelo, expressing regret, started the conversation, "I'm sorry for the inconvenience, sir, but I must say he definitely took the chain from me, even though he now dishonestly denies it."

The Second Merchant, curious about Antipholus's standing in the community, asked, "What's his reputation in this city?"

Angelo replied, emphasizing Antipholus's esteemed status, "He's highly respected, sir, with an excellent reputation and beloved by many. His word alone could guarantee any amount of my wealth at any time."

The Second Merchant, urging caution, whispered, "Speak quietly; I believe he's approaching."

As Antipholus of Syracuse and Dromio of Syracuse entered, Angelo pointed out, "There he is, wearing the very chain he vehemently denied having. Let me speak to him."

Approaching Antipholus, Angelo expressed his dismay, "Signior Antipholus, I'm surprised you'd bring me such shame and trouble, denying the chain you're now wearing so publicly, despite the oaths you made. You've not only wronged me but also this honest man here, delaying his departure."

Antipholus of Syracuse, caught off guard, responded, "I remember receiving a chain, but I never denied it."

The Second Merchant interjected, "But you did deny it, and you even swore falsely."

Antipholus questioned, "Who heard me deny or swear falsely?"

The Second Merchant, affirming his witness, retorted, "I did, and it's disgraceful that you continue to deceive in the company of honest people."

Antipholus of Syracuse, feeling accused, defended himself, "You're the one at fault for accusing me. I'm ready to prove my honesty and honor against your accusations if you dare to confront me."

The Second Merchant, filled with defiance, challenged, "I'm ready to stand against you. You're nothing but trouble."

As they drew their swords, ready to confront each other, Adriana, Luciana, the Lady, and others hurried onto the scene.

Adriana, in a panic, pleaded, "Stop, please don't hurt him! He's not himself; he's confused. Someone, grab his sword, and let's secure Dromio too. We need to take them to my place."

Dromio of Syracuse, sensing the urgency and danger, urged his master, "We need to find shelter, now! This looks like a safe place. Let's go inside quickly, or we're in big trouble!"

They quickly retreated into the Priory for safety. Just then, the Lady Abbess, Aemelia, appeared, surprised by the commotion.

"Why is everyone gathered here so frantically?" Aemelia inquired, seeking calm amid the chaos.

Adriana, desperate for help, explained, "We're here to get my husband. He's been acting so strangely, and we need to secure him for his own safety."

Angelo added, "It's clear he's not thinking straight."

The Second Merchant, regretting his earlier aggression, admitted, "I feel bad for drawing my sword on him now."

Aemelia, curious about the situation, asked, "How long has he been like this?"

Adriana detailed, "He's been off for a week—moody and not himself. But today, it got really bad."

"Has he lost money at sea, or is he grieving over someone? Or has he been distracted by someone else?" Aemelia probed further, trying to understand the root of the problem.

Adriana confessed, "It's the last one—he's been drawn away by someone."

Aemelia suggested that Adriana should have corrected him for that.

"I did," Adriana assured her.

"Yes, but perhaps not sternly enough," Aemelia implied, hinting at a firmer approach to the situation.

Adriana defended her actions, "I was as firm as I could be without compromising my dignity."

Aemelia suggested, "Perhaps you addressed it in private?"

"And in public too," Adriana added, indicating she didn't shy away from the issue.

Aemelia, however, thought it wasn't enough, "But perhaps not forcefully enough."

Adriana explained the extent of her efforts, "I didn't let the topic go, whether we were alone or with others. I constantly reminded him that his actions were wrong."

Aemelia interpreted the situation, "So, his distress might stem from the constant criticism. Continuous complaints can be more harmful than physical ailments. It seems your constant disapproval disrupted his peace, leading to his current state. Criticizing his actions, disturbing his meals and leisure—these actions could upset anyone, driving them to distraction."

Luciana interjected, defending Adriana, "She always spoke to him gently, even when he was out of line."

"Why don't you respond to these accusations?" Luciana asked Adriana, who felt cornered by her own arguments.

Adriana, feeling the weight of Aemelia's judgment, conceded, "It seems I've argued myself into a corner. Let's bring him out here."

Aemelia stood firm, "No one will be taken from this sanctuary, not until I've attempted to restore his sense, or else all efforts would be in vain. This place offers him protection, and he'll stay here until he recovers."

Adriana, steadfast in her resolve, declared, "I want to care for my husband, nurse him back to health myself. I don't need anyone else to do it for me. Please, let me take him home."

Aemelia, however, urged patience, "I must insist on keeping him here until I've tried all the treatments I know—medicinal syrups, drugs, and prayers to restore his health. It's part of my duty, my commitment to helping others."

Adriana refused to back down, "I cannot leave without him. It doesn't seem right for you to keep a husband away from his wife."

Aemelia remained firm, "You must leave now. He cannot go with you." With that, she exited, leaving the others behind.

Luciana suggested a course of action, "Let's take this matter to the duke. He should hear of what's happened."

Adriana, determined, agreed, "Yes, let's go to him. I won't rest until the duke has come to resolve this situation himself and ensures my husband is returned to me."

The Second Merchant, noting the time, mentioned, "It looks like it's about five o'clock. The duke is expected to pass by here soon to attend an execution at the melancholy vale just beyond the abbey."

Angelo, curious, asked, "For what reason?"

The Second Merchant explained, "A merchant from Syracuse faces execution for entering the city against its laws."

As they noticed the duke approaching with his entourage, including the condemned Syracusian merchant, Aegon, Angelo suggested, "Let's watch what happens."

Luciana advised, "We should kneel before the duke as he comes by."

As Duke Solinus appeared with Aegon and the execution party, he made a final announcement, "If anyone can pay the sum owed, this man's life will be spared. We wish to show him mercy if possible."

Adriana, seeking justice, appealed to Duke Solinus, "I must protest against the abbess for keeping my husband!"

The Duke, knowing the abbess's reputation, responded, "She's known for her virtue and reverence. It's hard to believe she'd wrong you."

Adriana pleaded her case, "Your Grace, my husband Antipholus, who I entrusted with everything upon your recommendation, has been seized by an uncontrollable madness today. He and his servant caused chaos, invading homes and taking whatever caught their fancy. I managed to restrain him once and sent him home to address the havoc he caused. But somehow, he escaped and, armed and furious, confronted us again. We sought help and when we tried to secure them once more, they fled into this abbey. The abbess refuses to release him or even let us see him. Please, command that he be released for his well-being."

Duke Solinus, recalling Antipholus's past service, assured her, "He once served me well, and I promised to support him. Let's summon the abbess to resolve this matter."

Just then, a servant rushed in with alarming news, "Mistress, you must act quickly! My master and his man have escaped; they've been causing mayhem, even setting the doctor's beard on fire and then trying to extinguish it with mud. They're out of control, and without intervention, they might harm the doctor severely."

Adriana, frustrated by the servant's interruption and misinformation, corrected him, "Be quiet! Both your master and his man are here, and your story is incorrect."

The servant, insistent and panicked, affirmed, "I swear it's true, mistress. I've barely caught my breath since witnessing it. He's out there, threatening harm if he catches you."

As cries were heard in the distance, the servant urged, "Listen! You must flee now!"

Duke Solinus, aiming to protect Adriana, assured her, "Stay close to me; there's nothing to fear." He signaled for guards to ready their weapons.

Adriana, distressed, exclaimed, "Oh, it must be my husband! It's unbelievable—he was just secured in the abbey, and now he seems to be elsewhere, beyond any logical explanation."

Just then, Antipholus of Ephesus and Dromio of Ephesus appeared, seeking the Duke's intervention.

Antipholus of Ephesus pleaded, "I ask for justice, Duke! Remember the service I rendered you in battle, the wounds I suffered to save your life. For that loyalty, I now seek your fairness."

Aegeon, recognizing his son and servant, wondered if his fear of impending death was causing hallucinations.

Antipholus of Ephesus continued, "I demand justice against that woman! She, whom you saw fit to be my wife, has wronged and dishonored me beyond measure today."

Duke Solinus, inclined to hear more, asked for specifics, "Explain the situation, and I'll judge fairly."

Antipholus accused Adriana of locking him out and entertaining others in his home, a serious allegation.

The Duke, shocked, turned to Adriana, "Is what he says true?"

Adriana firmly denied the accusations, "Absolutely not, my lord. He dined with me and my sister today. I swear by my soul, his accusations are baseless."

Luciana stepped forward to support Adriana's claim, "I swear by all that's holy, she's telling the truth to your highness!"

Angelo, however, labeled them deceitful, "They're both liars. This man's accusations against them are justified."

Antipholus of Ephesus appealed to the Duke, insisting on his clarity and sobriety, "My lord, I'm fully aware of what I'm saying, not influenced by wine or anger, though the wrongs done to me would drive a lesser man to madness. Today, this woman denied me entry to my own home for lunch. Angelo here, had he not been conspiring with her, could attest to that since he was supposed to bring a chain to me at the Porpentine, where I dined without him. When he failed to show, I went looking for him and ended up being falsely accused by him of receiving a chain I never saw, leading to my arrest. I sent my servant for money to secure my release, but he returned empty-handed. Then, in an attempt to clear this up, I encountered my wife, her sister, and their unsavory associates, along with a dubious character named Pinch, who claimed to be a conjurer. They overpowered me, and I was left bound in a dark cell until I managed to escape and came directly here, seeking justice for the humiliations I've endured."

Angelo confirmed to the Duke, "Indeed, he was locked out and did not dine at home."

Duke Solinus, seeking clarity, asked, "But did he receive a chain from you?"

Angelo affirmed, "Yes, my lord, he did have the chain. When he entered here, everyone saw it around his neck."

The Second Merchant added his testimony, "I even heard Angelo admit he gave the chain to Antipholus, despite initially denying it, which led to our confrontation right before he sought refuge in this abbey."

Antipholus of Ephesus contested these claims, "I've never entered these abbey walls before this moment, nor did we ever cross swords. I swear I've never seen the chain they accuse me of taking."

Duke Solinus, puzzled by the conflicting stories, commented, "This is quite the confusing accusation. It's as if everyone's been enchanted. If Antipholus was here, as claimed, why the confusion? His plea doesn't sound like the ravings of a madman. Yet, there's disagreement over where he dined and the ownership of the chain."

Turning to Dromio of Ephesus for his input, "What's your account?"

Dromio insisted, "He dined at the Porpentine, not at home."

The Lady chimed in, "He did, and he took a ring from my finger then."

Antipholus of Ephesus admitted to the Duke, "It's true; I received this ring from her."

The Duke, trying to make sense of the situation, asked the Lady, "Did you see him enter the abbey?"

"Yes, as clearly as I see you now, my liege," she asserted.

The Duke, more perplexed, ordered, "Fetch the abbess. This mystery deepens, and I suspect we're all being misled."

At that moment, Aegon seized the opportunity to speak, "Mighty Duke, may I say something? I believe I see someone here who could save my life by settling my debt."

Aegeon, given the chance to speak by Duke Solinus, asked, "Isn't your name Antipholus? And isn't this your assistant, Dromio?"

Dromio of Ephesus responded, "I was his assistant until an hour ago. He managed to free me from my ties. Now, I'm just Dromio, free from any bonds."

Aegeon, hopeful for recognition, said, "I'm sure both of you remember me."

Dromio replied, "We remember who we are, thanks to you. But you're not here as a patient of Doctor Pinch, are you?"

Aegeon, confused by their lack of recognition, pressed, "Why do you look at me as if I'm a stranger? You must know who I am."

Antipholus of Ephesus admitted, "I've never seen you before in my life."

Aegeon, saddened, mentioned, "Sorrow has changed me since you last saw me. Time has marked my face with its harsh touch, but don't you recognize my voice?"

Antipholus of Ephesus firmly said, "No, I don't."

Dromio also denied recognizing him, "Me neither, sir."

Aegeon insisted, "I'm certain you do."

Dromio humorously remarked, "Well, sir, even if you think so, I'm sure I don't. We have to believe what people say about themselves, right?"

Aegeon lamented, "Can it be that in just a few years, my voice has changed so much that my own son doesn't know me? Despite the changes in my appearance and the cold that seems to have taken over me, I still remember. I know you are my son, Antipholus."

Antipholus of Ephesus firmly stated, "I've never met my father in my life."

Aegeon, trying to jog his memory, replied, "But it's been seven years since we last saw each other in Syracuse. Maybe you're embarrassed to acknowledge me now that I'm in this condition."

Antipholus of Ephesus countered, "Everyone in the city can vouch for me; I've never been to Syracuse."

Duke Solinus intervened, "For twenty years, I've known Antipholus here in Ephesus, and he's never once visited Syracuse. Your age and distress are clouding your judgment."

At that moment, Aemilia entered with Antipholus and Dromio of Syracuse, causing a stir among the onlookers.

Adriana, shocked, exclaimed, "I can't believe my eyes; do I see two husbands?"

Duke Solinus, equally bewildered, wondered, "Which of these men is real, and which is the reflection? It's hard to tell them apart."

Dromio of Syracuse, trying to clarify, said, "I'm Dromio; he should leave."

Dromio of Ephesus protested, "No, I'm Dromio; I should stay."

Antipholus of Syracuse, seeing Aegeon, asked, "Is that you, Aegeon, or just his ghost?"

Dromio of Syracuse recognized Aegeon, "My old master! Who has captured you?"

Aemilia, determined to resolve the situation, declared, "It doesn't matter who tied him up; I'll set him free. Aegeon, if you are the man who once had a wife named Aemilia and two sons, speak to me, your Aemilia!"

Aegeon, filled with hope, asked Aemilia about their son who was with her on the raft during the shipwreck.

Aemilia recounted their separation, "We were rescued by people from Epidamnum, but fishermen from Corinth forcefully took my son and Dromio away, leaving me behind. I've been through much since then, leading to my current state."

Duke Solinus, piecing the story together, realized, "This matches Aegeon's account of the shipwreck. These two sets of twins, both Antipholuses and both Dromios, must be the children separated by fate."

Turning to Antipholus of Syracuse, he asked, "Did you arrive here from Corinth?"

Antipholus of Syracuse clarified, "No, my lord, I came from Syracuse."

Confused, Duke Solinus admitted, "I can't tell you two apart."

Antipholus of Ephesus then stated, "I was the one who came from Corinth, along with him," pointing to Dromio of Ephesus.

Adriana, trying to understand which Antipholus dined with her, asked, "Which one of you was at my table today?"

Antipholus of Syracuse answered, "It was me, ma'am."

Confused, Adriana asked, "Aren't you my husband?"

Antipholus of Ephesus firmly denied, "No, I am not the one you dined with."

This revelation started to unravel the confusion of identities, as everyone began to understand the extraordinary mix-up involving two sets of twins.

Antipholus of Syracuse acknowledged the confusion, "She did call me by your name, and her sister treated me as a brother." Turning to Luciana, he hinted at a future where he could explain everything, "I hope to clarify what I said before, now that this mix-up is coming to light."

Angelo identified the chain on Antipholus of Syracuse, "That's the chain you got from me."

Antipholus of Syracuse admitted, "Yes, it seems to be; I won't deny having it."

Antipholus of Ephesus pointed out, "And because of that chain, you had me arrested."

Angelo confirmed, "Yes, I believe that was the case; I can't deny it."

Adriana, trying to solve another piece of the puzzle, mentioned, "I sent bail money for you through Dromio, but it seems he didn't deliver it."

Dromio of Ephesus admitted, "I didn't bring any money."

Antipholus of Syracuse then realized, "I received a purse of ducats from you, and my Dromio brought it to me. It seems we've been mistaking each other's servants, leading to all these misunderstandings."

Antipholus of Ephesus, looking to resolve at least one issue, offered, "I'll use these ducats to bail out my father."

Duke Solinus, moved by the unfolding family reunion, announced, "There's no need for that; your father's life is spared."

The Lady, not wanting to be forgotten, reminded, "I still expect the diamond you promised me."

Antipholus of Ephesus, settling his debts, handed over the diamond, "Here, take it, and thank you for the hospitality."

Aemilia invited the Duke, "Please, come with us to the abbey to understand our full story. Everyone here, affected by today's mix-up, is welcome to join us for a feast to celebrate the resolution of this long-standing mystery."

The Duke agreed, "I'd be delighted to join this celebration."

After the crowd dispersed, Dromio of Syracuse asked Antipholus of Ephesus, "Shall I go get your belongings from the ship?"

Antipholus of Ephesus was confused, "What belongings of mine did you take to the ship?"

Dromio of Syracuse explained, "The goods you left at the inn, sir."

Realizing the mix-up, Antipholus of Syracuse said, "He's talking to me. Let's all go together and sort this out. And take a moment to embrace your brother, rejoice in finding each other."

With the two sets of twins reunited, they exited to celebrate their newfound relationships.

Dromio of Syracuse joked about the woman who mistook him for her husband, "She thought I was you at lunch. She'll be like a sister now, not a wife."

Dromio of Ephesus, amused, said, "It's like looking into a mirror with you. Ready to join the others and enjoy the feast?"

Dromio of Syracuse suggested, "You lead the way; you're the elder."

Dromio of Ephesus proposed, "Why not walk side by side, just as we entered the world together?"

With that, they left hand in hand, ending their adventure on a note of unity and brotherhood.

THE END

# "THE COMEDY OF ERRORS": A WHIRLWIND ADVENTURE OF MISTAKEN IDENTITIES AND UNFORESEEN FRIENDSHIPS

**An Urban Maze**: Crafted by William Shakespeare in the early 1590s, "The Comedy of Errors" stands as an exuberant narrative that intertwines elements of farce, romance, and slapstick within the bustling streets of Ephesus. The story kicks off with two sets of twins, Antipholus of Syracuse and Antipholus of Ephesus, along with their servants, both named Dromio, separated at birth by a shipwreck. Unbeknownst to them, their paths converge in Ephesus, setting the stage for a series of mistaken identities and comic misunderstandings.

**The Tangle of Mistaken Identities**: The core of the play revolves around the confusion sown by the presence of the two sets of twins in the same city. This premise acts as both a source of humor and a catalyst for the ensuing chaos, driving the narrative forward through a series of comedic mishaps and encounters that question the nature of identity and the bonds of familial ties.

**The Quest for Reunion**: At its heart, the play is a quest for reunion, as the separated family members navigate the labyrinth of their mirrored identities in search of each other. This journey not only provides the framework for the comedy but also underscores the play's exploration of themes such as the importance of family, the search for belonging, and the joy of rediscovery.

**Romantic Entanglements**: Amid the comedic turmoil, the play also weaves in strands of romance, notably between Antipholus of Syracuse and Luciana, sister to Antipholus of Ephesus's wife. These romantic entanglements add a layer of complexity to the play, highlighting the interplay between love, deception, and the pursuit of happiness.

**The Dynamics of Servitude and Friendship**: The Dromios, serving as the loyal servants and comedic relief, illuminate the themes of servitude, loyalty, and friendship. Their misadventures and witty exchanges not only contribute to the humor but also reflect on the human condition, emphasizing the value of companionship and understanding.

**Themes of Confusion and Resolution**: Through its intricate plot and character interactions, "The Comedy of Errors" delves into the confusion inherent in human relationships, the folly of assumptions, and the eventual triumph of truth and reconciliation, showcasing the restorative power of clarity and the reestablishment of order.

**Ephesus as a Convergence Point:** The setting of Ephesus acts as a crucible for the mix of characters and plots, serving as a backdrop that reflects the cultural and commercial vibrancy of the city while facilitating the play's explorations of identity, hospitality, and the universality of human folly.

**The Play Within a Play**: Shakespeare employs meta-theatrical elements to highlight the theatricality of the characters' predicaments, engaging the audience in a reflection on the nature of performance and the thin line between reality and perception.

**Shakespeare's Mastery of Comedy**: Regarded as one of Shakespeare's earliest and most lively comedies, "The Comedy of Errors" demonstrates his skillful handling of comedic timing, plot complexity, and character development, all while engaging with themes of love, confusion, and the joy of reunion.

**A Celebration of Human Absurdity and Affection**: Through its vibrant blend of mistaken identities, comedic escapades, and heartfelt reunions, "The Comedy of Errors" invites audiences into a world where every confusion paves the way for laughter and every resolution heralds the warmth of human connection, emphasizing the enduring charm of Shakespeare's comedic genius.

# THE LIFE OF WILLIAM SHAKESPEARE

Step back in time with us as we discover the exciting life of **William Shakespeare**—a storyteller whose magnificent tales have been told and retold for hundreds of years. Fasten your seatbelts for some amazing facts about the Bard of Avon!

**Birthday Mystery:** Believe it or not, we don't know exactly when Shakespeare was born. Historians guess it was around April 23, 1564, but that's all because of the date of his baptism. How curious that such a famous person has a birthday shrouded in mystery!

**School Days:** Young Shakespeare attended the King's New School in his hometown, where he learned important subjects like Latin, Greek, history, and poetry—all without the gadgets and technology students have today.

**Word Wizard:** Shakespeare had a way with words, inventing over 1,700 of them! Imagine, every time you say "bedroom" or "excitement," you're using words that Shakespeare introduced to the English language.

**Globe Trotter - But Not Really:** The Globe Theatre is where Shakespeare's masterpieces were first performed—not a globe you can spin, but a large, round, open-air theater where audiences marveled under the sky.

**Super-sized Works:** Our dear Bard wrote 37 plays and 154 sonnets. That's a lot of storytelling! If you wrote a poem every week of the year, you'd still be short of Shakespeare's sonnet count.

**Nicknamed "The Bard":** Shakespeare is often referred to as "The Bard of Avon." 'Bard' means poet, and indeed, Shakespeare was a master poet from the town of Stratford-upon-Avon.

**Lovey-Dovey Lines:** Shakespeare's words about love are so beautiful that they are still read at weddings and shared between sweethearts today. And if you've heard the phrase "to be or not to be," you're quoting one of his most famous lines!

**Queen for a Fan:** Queen Elizabeth I loved the theater, and Shakespeare's plays were some of her most enjoyed performances. It was quite the honor for Shakespeare to entertain her majesty with his work.

**Shakespeare's Secret Code:** Some folks believe that Shakespeare tucked away secret codes within his plays—making each performance not just a show, but also a puzzle full of hidden meanings.

**Goodnight, Sweet Prince:** At age 52, in the year 1616, Shakespeare took his final bow. His presence may be missed, but his stories live on, continuing to inspire, entertain, and provoke thought across the globe.

So there you have it—a little peek into the life of the man who has kept us company through his words for over four centuries. Open the pages of his stories, and let William Shakespeare's plays transport you to a world where imagination knows no bounds. Happy reading!

# ABOUT THE AUTHOR

Jeanette Vigon is a vibrant storyteller hailing from the sun-kissed beaches of California, where her Spanish heritage infuses her writing with a colorful zest for life. Born to Spanish immigrants who carried stories of their homeland across the ocean, Jeanette's childhood was rich with tales that sparked her imagination and sowed the seeds for her future in storytelling.

After completing her education with a focus on early childhood development, Jeanette dedicated herself to the noble profession of teaching. As a beloved primary school teacher, she spent years enlightening young minds in the classroom. Her magical ability to turn even the most mundane lesson into a memorable adventure earned her admiration from both her pupils and peers.

However, the call of the pen proved too strong for Jeanette to ignore. Diving headfirst into the world of literature, she transitioned from shaping minds with chalk to enchanting them with words as a full-time writer. Her intimate knowledge of children's learning styles, combined with her rich cultural roots, enables her to craft stories that are not only engaging but also educational.

Jeanette's writing is characterized by its empathy, humor, and a deep understanding of what captivates children's hearts and minds. Whether retelling a classic Shakespearean tale or penning an original story, her books are beloved for their ability to bridge cultural gaps and bring diverse experiences to the forefront of children's literature.

Now, with several acclaimed titles to her name, Jeanette continues to share her passion for enriching young lives through reading. When she's not lost in her latest manuscript, you can find her indulging in her love for travel, exploring new destinations, and collecting fresh inspirations for her next enchanting narrative.

It's hard for books to get noticed these days. Whether you liked this one or not, please consider writing a review, thanks!